About the author

Eugene Broxton was born in 1955 in Louisiana, USA.

In May 1991, he was arrested, charged with robbery and sentenced to death. Since then he has been sitting on death row in Texas, struggling to prove his innocence. Meanwhile, his lawyer Cathryn C. has requested his immediate release based on the results of the DNA test, but the fight is not yet over.

During the years of imprisonment Eugene Broxton wrote numerous poems that testify to despair, sadness, horror, but also to joy, hope and friendship.

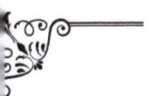

Innocent On Death Row
Poems by
Eugene Broxton

Freaky Sparrow Ltd.
1-4-3-24-7-365

Bibliografische Information der Deutschen Nationalbibliothek:
Die Deutsche Nationalbibliothek verzeichnet diese Publikation in der
Deutschen Nationalbibliografie; detaillierte bibliografische Daten sind
im Internet über http://dnb.dnb.de abrufbar.

Herstellung und Verlag: BoD – Books on Demand, Norderstedt

ISBN: 978-3-7460-3549-9

Table of Contents

Prolog 7

A friend like you 9

Death Row 11

Alone with Space 13

Back home again 15

Judge Ye not 17

Free 19

Niggers' Response to a Black Man's Death 21

God 23

Not a dream 25

I give thanks 27

Understand 29

Lady 31

Joseph Lave 33

You are my best friend 35

In your eyes 37

Luck 39

Be a friend today 41

Goodbye 43

PROLOG

In the years that I have known Eugene Broxton I have been impressed by his positive outlook. Imagine withstanding the condescending and demeaning treatment meted out daily for twenty five years while maintaining a sense of dignity, self respect, and compassion even for those that show coarse insensitivity to him. I have been equally impressed by his fine mind, that he taught himself to read after his incarceration and that he now writes beautiful letters that bristle with complex sentences. In addition Eugene maintains very lively connections through his correspondence with friends all over the world. These accomplishments must rank among the highest human achievements and have been an inspiration to me. I should add that I value the time I have been able to spend visiting with Eugene as he always has interesting and touching stories to tell about his life. His personal warmth and good humor are delightful to behold. In my portrait of him I endeavored capture these fine qualities.

November 2017, Peter Charlap

A FRIEND LIKE YOU

It's nice to have a friend like you
With whom my heart can share
Its little hopes and fondest dreams
Because you really care.

It's good to know I need but call
In case my foot should slip.
You're like a lighthouse in the fog
That guides my little ship.

It's nice to have a friend like you
Within this 'vale of tears'.
Someone who never changes
However long the years.

...

Who sees beyond the features
And all the outward show,
And needs no words to read the thoughts
That only friends can know.

It's nice to have a friend like you,
Forever and a day.
Who through the good times and the bad
Will never go away.

No matter what the future holds,
Whatever life may send.

I'll always know I have been blessed
Because you are my friend.

DEATH ROW

The bars are blue and walls are white.
I set here in this cell with yet nothing else to do
again tonight!
Red bricks and steel grey fence, - that all I can see
when I look out the window …
I hear of birds sing, a man laughter or even a scream.
Guard in gray some are black, some white, they are
part of who took my freedom away. – This place I am
and where grass nor flowers grow, a human slaughter
House, - they call Death Row!
I've did some crimes, and I've did a few, but now
they want to take my life for a crime I didn't do!

…

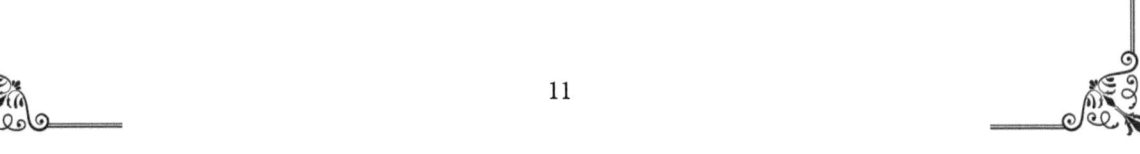

...

They call it justice, but they mean just us poor and
there's quite a few Feeling helpless, come times
Hopeless too, -- I don't know what more to do –
Wanting to cry at times evening wanting to die ...
Struggling to keep my sanity, desiring to be free!
The State murdering us the poor and there quite a few
And they call it justice but they mean just us, --
And there's quite a few.
And there's nothing I can do!

ALONE WITH SPACE

When I reach out across the empty land
To the far and lonely sky,
I see you miraged in a special place
Where only eagles fly.
And when I stop to think of what
You may have been
The mirage clears before my eyes,
Like touching paradise.
But now I am alone with space
Where feelings turn around
And make me cry out loud
Where not a single soul can hear.

BACK HOME AGAIN

Some urging within me keeps calling
For me to come home just one more time.
My thoughts travel to faraway places,
To the land where I'd been long before.
My faltering steps prevent wandering.
So only in dreams can I flee.
In this cage I sit and remember
Its the place where I want to be.
Tonight I will walk in the moonlight
Listening to the sounds close by;
On the grass dew gleams like diamonds
As if stars had fallen from the sky.

...

...

I will think of the home of my childhood
To the place I still hold most dear,
As I close my eyes and remember,
The memories flood back all to clear.

I can feel the sun and soft breezes,
The smell of my Momma's cooking
I imagine the days of my childhood
With the magic of dreams long gone by.

JUDGE YE NOT

Have you walked in the shoes
Of the person you judge,
Have you shared their most
Intimate thoughts,
Have you known of the tears,
The doubts and the fears,
Or the battle that person
Has fought?
Have you shared in the secrets
That lie in the heart,
Of the one you unjustly accuse?
If you haven't don't criticize
Judge or condemn
Unless you have walked in their shoes!

...

When they don't understand,
They condemn off hand ...
But trusting in me,
Your eyes confide,
Holding nothing,
Telling no lies,
Then suddenly I was startled,
At my own reflection,
Your eyes mirrored
My imperfection,
So, who was I looking at?
Who did I really see?
Was it you?
Or was it me?
Or am I you?

And you are me?

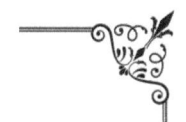

Free

Anthony Graves I know the pain and
anguish he felt as he set here on Texas
death row. Eighteen years deprived of life and
freedom, 18 years of wondering would he
ever go free, or be executed like so many
others. Deprived of all life pleasures and
joy. But in many ways he was lucky to
go free after 18 years of madness he
had to endure and see, Eighteen years
of lonely nights, 18 years of tears, 18 years
of fear and worries. And one point four
million dollars isn't enough to set him
free. But I hope with all my heart and soul
that Anthony can get pass all that he went
through and live happily and eventually
truely be free. I only wish after 20 years
it will happen for me, I am innocent
too and like Anthony no one believe me.

Nigger's Response
To A Black Man's Death

Pow!
Rifle bullet to the head
Pow!
Shot that King nigger dead
Pow!
White boy lurking somewhere's about
Pow!
Took that Evern nigger out
Pow!
Shotgun slug to the chest
Pow!
Laid Malcolm's ass to rest
Pow!
Fool as nigger shudda stayed quiet
Pow!

...

...
Didn't think justice could be denied
Pow!
Nigger dead now and cannot see
Pow!
That '44 is '63
Pow!
Things don't change in the U.S.A.
Pow!
Not for us Nigger, anyway

God

I saw God today, He was the
clouds, moving across the earth
He was not in a hurry,
And was at peace ...

I saw God again, He was the
ocean, and He was the sea.
As calm as could he.
Tranquillity was all around.

God was the wind and the sky
as far as human eyes could see.
We see God every day.
I wonder does God ever see me?

Not A Dream

Sometimes I want to cry and scream.
I want to get out of this nightmare,
Because this isn't my dream.
I did nothing to deserve to be tortured
And the madness I have to deal with
From day to day.

I see the executioner when he passes by this cage,
As he looks in on me and smiles.
He asks *'How are you doing?'*
I say I am making it.
I watch him as he walks away.
This is a nightmare, it's not my dream.

...

I have been stuck here twenty-five years now.
I've seen over 500 men they have taken
To the death chamber.

Yes, I want to cry and scream.
I know this isn't a dream.
I wonder, will the executioner get me
Before it's over with?
I want to say I don't care,
But that wouldn't be true.

I do want this nightmare over with.
I wish for that to come true.
This is not a dream.

I Give Thanks

For all the peaceful hours I have enjoyed.
I give thanks.
For all the troubled hours I have endured with strength,
I give thanks.
For all the beauty I have seen,
I give thanks.
For the food that fed my body & soul,
I give thanks.
For friendships gone & those to come,
I give thanks.
For those who loved me when I needed love the most,
I give thanks.
For the courage to face the days ahead with hope,
I give Thanks!!

Understand

I don't understand when fire sweep across
The land and waters wash away the sand.
And leave misery and disaster in its wake.
Sometimes there is lost of lives
And we ask God why,
And we get no answers.
Some of us are fortunate, and can
Rebuild and start a new.
Many take decades, and some never do
Get back on their feet.

My tragedies was not made by nature
Or as we call it; acts of God
Men told lies on me
That sent me not only to the penitentiary
I'm on death row for a murder I didn't do.

...

And like with all tragic events,
I asked God why and I got no answer
I still hang on to hope and some how
I still have my sanity, I haven't gotten
Out of the water nor fire
I don't know if this be the end of me
Life is weird, and sometimes we never
Understand why things happen as it do.

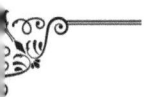

LADY

When I was a child,
I had a dog
I called her Lady
She loved me like no other,
I loved her too
She stayed by my side
And tried to protect me,
And went with me everywhere I'd go.
My Mom had Lady taken away from me
I never saw Lady any more
Yes I was heart broken
I still miss Lady today
That was more than 50 years ago.

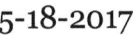

JOSEPH LAVE

10-17-1964   5-18-2017

Joe Lave. Joo Lave, man I hate you had
to leave this way ... it seems,
I just saw you yesterday
Now I was told you died
Man Joe that took my breath away.
A young man, you was only 52
We met 22 years ago
and even though over the years
We didn't see each other often
But man you had become family to me
a little brother, a damn good friend
And out of nowhere your life has
come to an end
If there is life after death,
Well you've gotten away from this mess.
My heart goes out to your family and
friends.
And my heart is broken because your
Life has came to an end.

You Are My Best Friend

You are my best friend
Because you feel so much
Like home to me ...
That feeling that someone cares:
That feeling of welcome
That the sight of home
Always brings.
With you as my friend,
I can always know sunshine
more than my troubles.
You turn my sadness
That I can accept ...
And when I'm feeling happy ...
And wanting to share,
Everything that is wonderful to me
You are there ... Ready to listen

IN YOUR EYES

Your heart light shines,
There're an humanitarian spirit,
A soul divine
Prefect in no way, And vulnerable I say
There's bleeding wounds,
From having dared loved
So courageous you are,
Yet meek as a dove,
With skeletons in your closet.
As do all of the living,
Afraid to be discovered,
By the unforgiving,
Because people can be cruel

LUCK

As a child I had no dreams
As a young man trying to figure
out what to be.
I ended up being sent to the penitentiary
Without no love and support
I struggled to make the best of life
But no one seemed to give me a chance
God know I'm telling the truth
How I ended up on death row
I have no cue, but I know
I didn't murder the person
A jury judged me guilty for
The justice system is a joke and
It damn sho don't work
If you can afford a lawyer
You have a chance
But if you are broke
You are shit out of luck.

GOODBYE

Saying goodbye is never easy
But moving on
We all must do
Going on with our lives
Not just talking about it
But seeing it through
Move on,
My love,
Move on,
And live,
You have,
Much more to give

...

...

Now it's time I must go
It's not easy to say good bye
But it's time
So I say good bye
Know my love for you is true
And as long as you live,
My love will be with you

BE A FRIEND TODAY

There always is a friend in need
Along life's lonely way
Don't count on him to ask you,
Just be there for him today.
Just knowing there is someone, is often
All it takes,
To lift a body's spirits,
And a loyal friendship makes.
A smile, a little laughter,
A letter that you send,
Can make a world of difference,
At a time one needs a friend.
An arm to proudly lean on,
In times of stress or strife,
Can truly be a blessing,
On the road we know as life!